The Nautical Hour

D1176755

By Tony Bailey

World Harvest Ministries
903 3rd Street NE
Puyallup, WA 98372

Design: Tony Bailey

For information write:
Tony Bailey
2510 North Expressway
Griffin, GA 30223

bailey@worldharvestministries.net
www.worldharvestministeries.net

Library of Congress Catalog-in-Publication Data
Bailey, Tony
The Nautical Hour / Tony Bailey
ISBN: 0-9728629-2-7

Dedication

The Nautical Hour is dedicated first, to the Lord Jesus Christ. To my pastor, Rev. B. S. Cole and to the many ministers, who arc too numerous to name, who have invested so much in my salvation and ministry. A special thanks and recognition to the one person who has had, and continues to have the greatest positive impact on my life and ministry; my most devoted admirer, my most consistent encourager, my dearest friend, and the one true love of my life, the Mother of my children, my darling wife, Karen.

Acknowledgements

Thanks to Karen, Tiffany & Ray, Crystal & Rusty, Alison & Brandon, for all of your support and encouragement while writing this book. Thank you for all of the times that you read it over and over helping to make corrections and adding little extras to make it special! You are my life and I love you all with all of my heart!

Thanks to Kit Mernick and Melissa Fross for your vision and the assistance in editing. It is greatly appreciated. And a huge "thank you" to Lizbeth Freeman for the final edition editing and the work on future endeavors.

Thank you to the saints in Griffin, who for the past eighteen years have been a consistent support in prayer and encouragement.

Thanks to the many ministerial friends and prayer warriors who have helped by adding so much to my understanding of prayer

Forward

So much could be written about the importance of the Nautical Hour as it applies to spiritual life. This writing is not an attempt to exhaust the subject of early morning prayer but to introduce the many scriptural examples, blessings and benefits derived from a dedicated effort to rise early in the morning for prayer. According to Jesus, the commitment of seeking Him first will bring into our lives all things of which we have need. Many years ago, a dear friend and respected colleague, passed along this advice: "Tony, you don't have to say everything that can be said at one time, just make sure you say enough." Hopefully I have.

Table of Contents

The Nautical Hour

Before the days of satellite guidance systems, navigation on the open sea took a great deal of skill and understanding. In order to point the ship in the desired heading, the navigator had to know more than where he desired to go, he had to know the ship's present location. Since no landmarks are visible on the open sea, stable points of reference had to be discovered before the navigator could accurately triangulate the ship's position. The night sky offered these reference points in the form of stars and celestial patterns. The navigator would study the stars and with a few simple calculations determine the approximant longitude and latitude of the ship. But the night sky offered no visible horizon toward which the ship could be directed. For the proper horizon to be found the navigator needed the light of day, which, with its arrival would wash away the visibility of the stars.

The Nautical Hour was soon discovered as the most crucial hour of the navigator's day. The only time of day when the stars of night and the horizon of the coming day were both visible to the navigator was the period of time before sunrise when night is changing into day. Once the sun was up the navigator lost the ability to calculate the location of the ship, but during the Nautical Hour, the navigator could determine not only the location of the ship but also the proper heading.

Often through the hectic schedules of our busy days, we can only point our ship in the direction of what appears to be the right horizon and hope for the best. At night, we are able to reflect on the day's events and decisions and to evaluate our present position. But, during that early hour before the rising of the sun we can determine both our position and direction if we are willing to spend time with Jesus. It is impossible to effectively determine our heading without knowing our present position. God has given us a time when we can come into His presence and discover not only our position in Him but where we can also chart our course in His chosen direction:

"The Nautical Hour"

When the Lord first began to deal with me about praying early in the morning, I resisted. I was, by my own reckoning, fairly successful as a minister. I was at that time pastoring my second church. Both of the churches to which God had brought me had witnessed significant growth rather quickly. Both of the churches had received national recognition as "The Fastest Growing Church" in North America.

Through my personal soul-winning efforts, over five hundred people had been won to the

Lord. I had been the featured speaker at many conferences, and there was a constant demand for me to teach seminars ranging in subject from "Church Growth" to "Family Relationship". I had served or been asked to serve on many committees and boards of both the ministerial fellowship with which I was involved and the city where I pastored. The Lord had opened up many gifts of the Spirit in my ministry. I had a consistent, established prayer-life and a daily Bible reading program, to which I was very faithful. I had a fairly clear vision of where I wanted to go in God, although I did not have a clue as to what else I could do to get there. I was working as hard for the Kingdom of God as anyone that I knew. I tried everything that anyone would suggest. My plate was full and I was bone tired most of the time, so, when the Lord asked me to get up early to pray, I resisted. I had, for as long as I remembered, been a "night person". When everyone else was settled and in bed, I would have my private time with God and His Word. It was easy for me to spend two or three hours in prayer every night. All-night prayer meetings were a common occurrence for me. But now God was asking me to change my whole life, again. I explained to God, (as if He did not know all things) that I was a "night person" and how hard it was for me to make this change.

God persisted. After much deliberation, I presented my closing argument, "God, I can't get up that early because I can't get to bed early enough." God countered, "If you start getting up early in the morning you'll find a way to get to bed early enough."

One of the first things that I noticed about getting up early to pray was the change in prayer itself. Previously, a great deal of my prayer had been filled with repentance. There had been a lot of weeping and a feeling of condemnation over not doing enough for God, (although I never knew what "enough" was). By changing my prayer time, the prayer itself changed because I did not have much to repent over at four o'clock in the morning.

My time in prayer became more productive simply by not having to spend so much of it recovering from some snare of the devil. Because I did not have to repent about opportunities missed, I could spend that time receiving directions for the day. I could clearly see the horizon for which I was heading in the Spirit, and for the first time in my life I could establish my position in the Spirit at the same time.

The Scripture admonishes all to be "followers of them who through faith and patience inherit the promises" (Hebrews 6:12). The word "followers" literally means, "to imitate", or "act in the same fashion or to pattern your life after." So, when reading about the lives and events of great men and women of God, believers should not only observe the lives of the patriarchs, but should also seek to imitate their lives as closely as possible. There seems to be no particular personality or character in God's choice of men and women who were called and empowered to work for His Kingdom. Some lived in a palace while others had no home at all. Some were educated by the highest standards of the day while others were deemed "ignorant and unlearned". The wealthy were called into God's service, as were the poor. At first glance, there seems to be no common thread that connects the diverse servants of the Lord. Indeed, there is nothing in the make-up or nature of these varied individuals that would place them in the same arena of God's call. There is, however, a common denominator in the lifestyles of these chosen vessels, one that can be duplicated by anyone desiring to be used of God. What is this singular element that unites the lives of those who have made a significant impact in this world for the Kingdom of God? Simply this: consistent, travailing prayer at daybreak. Some might call this "effectual, fervent prayer."

Jesus himself gives a very candid explanation of how to be chosen for God's use: "For the kingdom of heaven is like unto a man that is an householder, which went out early in the morning to hire laborers into his vineyard" (Matthew 20:1). The phrase "the kingdom of heaven is like" should catch the attention of any Kingdom-minded Christian. The words following that phrase should be of the utmost importance to anyone desiring to please God. Jesus said that in his Kingdom, He looks before the sun ever comes up for someone whom He will use that day. If anyone truly desires to be used of God, he or she must get out of bed and get down to the labor pool by dawn.

Neither the lazy, nor "sleepy-heads", will inherit God's promises (see Proverbs 6:9-11, 19:15, 20:13, Hebrew 6:12).

It must be stated here that the vast majority of Church culture is anti-revival. In order to accommodate a greater manifestation of God, we must change our lifestyle. Changing priorities is a choice that we must willingly make as disciples who are determined to be of use to God. The Church's greatest need is not so much for a move of the Spirit as it is for a removal of carnality. God has warned his Church of the spiritual atmosphere in the last days. The Apostle Paul even refers to the last days in his writings to Timothy:

> *"Now the Spirit speaketh expressly, that in the latter times some shall depart from the faith, giving heed to seducing spirits, and doctrines of devils; speaking lies in hypocrisy; having their conscience seared with a hot iron"* (I Timothy 4:1-2).

> *"This know also, that in the last days, perilous times shall come. For men shall be lovers of their own selves, covetous, boasters, proud, blasphemers, disobedient to parents, unthankful, unholy, without natural affection, trucebreakers, false accusers, incontinent, fierce, despisers of those that are good, traitors, heady, highminded, lovers of pleasures more than lovers of God;*

having a form of godliness, but denying the power thereof: from such turn away. For of this sort are they which creep into houses, and lead captive silly women laden with sins, led away with divers lusts, ever learning and never able to come to the knowledge of the truth" (II Timothy 3:1-7).

With all of the "spiritual wickedness in high places" in these "perilous times", and with all of the evils of both human and demonic spirits abounding, it is imperative that God's Church rediscovers both the place and position of early morning prayer.

The Psalmist gives insight to a place in prayer where God's people have not only the authority and power, but also the right and ability to use that authority. By aligning oneself with the Word of God, any Believer can pray with confidence and bind evil spirits and influences, both human and demonic, according to Psalm 49. That place of prayer is at the break of day. "The upright shall have dominion over them in the morning" (Psalm 49:14). As the light of the world, Christians should usher in each new day and release Godly influence to have total dominion.

Over the past fifteen years of practicing early morning prayer, there have been storms that have come to my life and knocked me off course. The tides of change and the currents of traditions have at various times turned me in the wrong direction. But, by consistently rising early to pray, I have been able to re-evaluate my position and re-chart my course to keep my life headed in the right direction.

The Word of God, personal experience, and the lives and testimonies of others, have caused me to understand that the most crucial hour of the day, for anyone desiring to be all that they can be in God, is the Nautical Hour.

Battlefield of the Mind

According to the voice of condemnation, no matter how much we pray, we never pray enough. With no clear scriptural definition of 'enough prayer', it is easy for the enemy to keep us convinced that we will always be reaching for, yet never obtaining, the promises of God. Discovering a place of total surrender and intimacy in the presence of Jesus each morning seems to answer the question of "enough prayer."

Condemnation is not of faith and is therefore sin. (Romans 14:23) Of course, it is not possible to have confidence in God when our heart is full of condemnation. (1 John 3:21) Until we allow God to totally transform our thinking habits and renew the spirit of our minds, we will continue to fall prey to the adversary. (Romans 12:2, Ephesians 4:23) However, the Word of God has promised that we can recover ourselves from the snare of the devil by acknowledging the truth. (2 Timothy 2:25-26) And the truth is: "There is therefore now no condemnation to them which are in Christ Jesus, who walk not after the flesh, but after the Spirit." (Romans 8:1)

The Word of God teaches several lessons about spiritual warfare, including the following:

> *"For though we walk in the flesh, we do not war after the flesh: (For the weapons of our warfare are not carnal, but mighty through God to the pulling down of strongholds;) Casting down imaginations, and every high thing that exalteth itself against the knowledge of God, and bringing into captivity every thought to the obedience of Christ; and having in a readiness to revenge all disobedience, when your obedience is fulfilled."* (II Corinthians 10:3-6)

According to this passage, there is, in fact, a war going on. That's lesson one. Lesson two says that God's people will not be victorious in this war by resorting to natural abilities and talents. If strongholds are to be pulled down, it will be by the use of spiritual equipment, which God has labeled as "mighty". Any believer can use God's spiritual weaponry to cast down imaginations, every high thing that may seek to exalt its own authority over God's authority and thoughts that are contrary to the Word of God. The spiritual weapons of our warfare are mighty, no matter how these "high things" present themselves: whether they are carnal, attitudinal, spiritual, political or of any other nature. (See Philippians 2:10) This text in II Corinthians also implies that the Church can now hold in captivity the powers that once held a person, family, city or place captive.

Notice also the believer's responsibility to assume the place of dominion within the jurisdiction of his or her spiritual authority in submission and obedience to the authority of Christ. Realization of the principlo of spiritual warfare is the beginning of entrance into battle. So many Christians spend the majority of their prayer time trying to root-out demonic strongholds in circumstances, situations and people that surround their life. Sad to say, but strongholds are not on the outside, they are internal. When addressing the subject of strongholds, the Apostle immediately went to the things within a believer that affects the reasoning process. It is through the process of reasoning that self-evaluation occurs and thus establishes as fact (whether true or not) a personal self-image. This personal evaluation is extremely dangerous to our self-image if strongholds still exist. Strongholds are developed by openly accepting as truth what the enemy says, when it is well established by the Word of God that "the truth is not in him." (John 8:44) In the Garden of Eden it was made clear that the devil would point out every failure of man for he is identified by God as, "the accuser of the brethren." (Revelation 12:10)

So, what causes most Christians to fall prey to the lies of the deceiver? It is, in a word, "shame." Unresolved shame in the life of a believer is the only doorway through which the devil can come. Shame creates a pattern of thought that defiles the reasoning process and therefore produces a tainted self-image. This is

21

why so many of God's children feel unworthy to approach their Heavenly Father in the confidence of His unconditional love for them. Since strongholds are erected in the mind they must be dealt with by the Word of God. The "sword of the Spirit" is the only weapon that can divide asunder the soul and the spirit of a man. (Hebrews 4:12) No one can hope to rightly divide the Word of Truth unless they have been rightly divided by the Word of Truth. Without first allowing the Word to do its full work in us, destroying strongholds that the thought pattern of shame has established, we cannot begin to walk in the full scope of the power of God.

After many years of living for God and being totally involved in full-time ministry, I was surprised by a vision of the Lord Jesus standing in my bedroom early one morning. He stood looking at me so lovingly and after a moment He spoke. "You need to be filled with my Spirit," He said. "Filled with Your Spirit" I thought, "I am filled with Your Spirit." Needless to say, after that encounter I could not sleep any longer, so I made my way into the den and fell on my knees in prayer. I began to weep and to remind God about my conversion experience. When I was through the same vision appeared again with the Lord saying the same thing, "You need to be filled with my Spirit." I wept harder and searched deeper praying God to show me what I needed to do to be saved. I rehearsed the years of commitment, study, dedication, ministry, and so forth, asking God to open my understanding. When I finished praying the same vision came for the third time with the same words, "You need to be filled with my Spirit." But this time an understanding came with the vision. Jesus was telling me that I needed to be filled with the "spirit of Christ." I was born-again and had been for many years but I had not allowed the mind, nature, and spirit of Christ to develop in me. I had to let God deal with the self-image that shame-based thinking had created.

Allowing God to deal with shame and its aftermath is not an experience. It is a life-long process. Through the years, I continue to be amazed at God's deliverance. Many attitudes and concepts that I had accepted as my own were actually false self-images that developed by accepting and believing the voice of shame. Once you have allowed God to begin healing and delivering you from shame, stay in the process, for only "he that endures until the end shall be made whole."

Nature of the Enemy

There is a struggle each and every day for authority and control in the spirit realm here on earth. God's will is established in heaven, but according to Jesus' response to the disciples' plea for instruction in prayer, it is the act of prayer by believers that settles God's will on earth. (See Luke 11:2). The answer to the question of "Who will rule the day?" may very well depend upon who shows up for the battle. If the Church presumes to "take the day" for Christ, it must send soldiers into the fray. It is not difficult to understand, but the manual, which is the Word of God, must be studied in order to take full advantage of the equipment that God has placed at His saints' disposal. We cannot afford to enter battle without knowing whom we will meet on the battlefield.

The prophet Isaiah sheds some light on the character of our enemy. The following are four different translations of Isaiah 14:12:

> *"How art thou fallen from heaven, O Lucifer, son of the morning! How art thou cut down to the ground, which didst weaken the nations!" (KJV)*

"How you have fallen from heaven, O star of the morning son of the dawn! You have been cut down to the earth, you who have weakened the nations!" (NAS)

"How you have fallen from heaven, O morning star, son of the dawn! You have been cast down to the earth, you who once laid low the nations!" (NIV)

"How art thou fallen from heaven, O day-star, son of the morning! How art thou cut down to the ground, that didst lay low the nations!" (ASV)

According to these translations of scripture, in the beginning, the enemy was created by God to be the very "offspring of the morning". Lucifer was "begotten by" or "given life by" the morning. This "son of the morning" ushered in each and every day. Lucifer preceded the rising of the sun. It was intended that he be the first light of each new day. God created him with a nature to rule the day. Though Lucifer may have been created to be the first light of day, his pride and rebellion led God to cast him into the earth which "was without form, and void; and darkness was upon the face of the deep." (Genesis 1:2) Even in this darkened state, Lucifer still projects himself as light, according to II Corinthians 11:14; "For Satan himself is transformed into an angel of light." God created him with the nature of light to have dominion over the day; therefore, the battle begins anew each morning. The authority (dominion) over light and day has been transferred from Lucifer to Christ.

"Through the tender mercy of our God; whereby the day-spring ['a rising up' or 'to cause to rise'] from on high hath visited us, to give light to them that sit in darkness and in the shadow of death, to guide our feet into the way of peace." (Luke 1:78-79; also see John 1:4-5, 9; John 8:12; John 9:5.)

Dominion over light has been transferred secondly to the Church through Christ's commission, "Ye are the light of the world" (Matthew 5:14; also see Eph.5:8). As the "light of the world", God's people should rule the day. After all, God has given man dominion over the same earth into which He cast Satan. "And God said, Let us make man in our image, after our likeness: and let them have dominion over the fish of the sea, and over the fowl of the air, and over the cattle, and over all the earth, and over every creeping thing that creepeth upon the earth. So God created man in his own image, in the image of God created he him; male and female created he them. And God blessed them, and God said unto them, be fruitful, and multiply, and replenish the earth, and subdue it: and have dominion over the fish of the sea, and over the fowl of the air, and over every living thing that moveth upon the earth." (Genesis 1:26-28; also see Psalms 8:4-6; Psalms 49:14; Romans 6:9, 14; and Ephesians 1:17-23.)

Lucifer may not be easily convinced, but the Word has declared God's Church as the new authority in the earth. The Lord promised, "Out of Jacob shall come he that shall have dominion, and shall destroy him that remaineth." (Numbers 24:19) Satan's power and influence has been destroyed by the death of Jesus on the cross and by His resurrection from the grave. "And having spoiled principalities and powers, he made a shew of them openly, triumphing over them in it." (Colossians 2:15; also see Ephesians 2:16; Philippians 2:8-10; Colossians 1:22)

From the beginning, it was God's intent that Lucifer should have his authority violently ripped from his hands by the "Saints of the Most High God". (See Revelation 13:8; Matthew 11:12.) God boldly proclaimed this plan in the book of The Beginnings: "And it shall come to pass when thou shalt have the dominion, that thou shalt break his yoke from off thy neck." (Genesis 27:40)

"My voice shalt thou hear in the morning O Lord; in the morning will I direct my prayer unto thee, and will look up." (Psalm 5:3)

The Hebrew word that is translated "direct" in the King James is actually defined as joining in the battle and putting in order. The word that is translated "morning" still means prior to the rising of the sun. It would be correct to translate this verse as: "My voice shalt thou hear before sunrise O Lord; before the rising of the sun will I join in the battle and order my steps in thee, and will look up." The Psalmist declares that his participation in the battle will be his prayer. The words that come out of his mouth in his morning prayer will establish the order of the day.

I had already been praying for three years against the demonic spirit that bound the city in which I was a pastor when God began to talk to me about early morning prayer. After much struggle I finally committed to praying at six o'clock in the morning. For the next few weeks, I was very faithful to my commitment to early morning prayer and I had noticed a wonderful change in the spirit of our city. One morning before my prayer time, I was awakened by a demonic spirit that was standing in my room. This demon spirit looked like a very large and intimidating man. He stood glaring at me silently for what seemed like minutes and then he spoke, "You may have defeated the prince of your city, but I'm here now." I simply stared back at him not really knowing how to respond. Then slowly I realized what he had said, or at least the part that mattered, "I had defeated the prince of my city." Not only had I defeated the spirit that had bound my city, that ignorant devil showed up to tell me the news. I then began to laugh out loud and said to that demonic spirit, "First of all, I didn't defeat the prince of this city, Jesus did, and He's defeated you too. Now get out of my house." I watched that spirit drop his head, slowly turn, and walk out.

A couple of nights later I was preaching a service in the southern part of our state. The Pastor and I went out for some fellowship after church and he began to tell me a story. He started by letting me know that nothing like this had ever happened to him before, and he did not want me to think that he was losing his mind. "Last night", he said, "a demon spirit came into my bedroom." At this point I interrupted him and said, "Let me tell you what he looked like." I began to describe the spirit that had come into my house a couple of nights before. As I described feature after feature his eyes got wider and wider. When I had completed my description the Pastor said, "There was just one difference. The spirit that came into my bedroom had a large bandage across his face."

The demonic spirit, which had held my city in bondage for years, was defeated by simply changing the time that I prayed. By standing on the authority of God's Word and involving myself in spiritual warfare, demonic principalities had to yield to my command. It is "forever settled in Heaven" that the righteous, have dominion over every unclean spirit at that time when night is changing into day. (Psalm 119:89 and Psalm 49:14) This same dominion belongs to every child of God.

Weapons of Our Warfare

In natural terms, the military never attempts to enter a battle unarmed. Why then does the Church? We must use the weapons of warfare that the Lord has provided. The spiritual arsenal, if it were listed, would begin and end with prayer. While it does not abide alone, prayer is one of the most powerful weapons available to the Church. In fact, prayer may be the single most powerful weapon against the enemy. Thus, we come to the theme of this discourse: prayer in and at its most effective level. After all, it is only "The effectual fervent prayer of a righteous man (that) availeth much." (James 5:16)

Why morning prayer? Spiritually speaking, the battle for the day must take place at the beginning of the day rather than the end. Why, then, do the greatest number of prayer meetings take place at night, after the day is spent, after the day is lost? Most nighttime prayers are by nature built around repentance for things done wrong and opportunities lost during the day. Night prayers include more weeping over oneself than weeping over the unharvested souls of men. One can see, then, that praying at night is like studying after a test, rather than before. You may learn the material, but you still have to repeat the course. It makes spiritual sense to fight for the day before the day begins.

In addition to the power of prayer, God has equipped His elect with His Word of truth (John 17:17). His Word builds faith in all who will hear (Romans 10:17). According to Ephesians 6:17, God's Word is the "sword of the spirit" that Hebrews 4:12 describes as "quick, and powerful, and sharper than any two-edged sword, piercing even to the dividing asunder of soul and spirit, and of the joints and marrow, and is a discerner of the thoughts and intents of the heart." Anyone who is willing to "receive with meekness the engrafted word" can be saved, "for it is the power of God unto salvation to every one that believeth" (James 1:21; Romans 1:16).

The Lord has given not only His Word as a weapon, but also the authority of His Name. "And these signs shall follow them that believe; In my name shall they cast out devils" (Mark 16:17). When we obey God's commandments, He has ordained that "even the devils are subject unto us through his name" (Luke 10:17). And, if we shall ask any thing in his name, He will do it (John 14:14). For, "neither is there salvation in any other: For there is none other name under heaven given among men, whereby we must be saved" (Acts 4:12). "God also hath highly exalted him, and given him a name which is above every name, that at the name of Jesus, every knee should bow, of things in heaven, and things in earth, and things under the earth" (Philippians 2:9-10; also see Matthew 1:21, 12:21).

Before Jesus ascended into the heavens, He promised that His followers would not be left to fend for themselves against the wiles of the devil. The shield of faith, which comes from the hearing of the word, quenches the fiery darts of the enemy (Ephesians 6:16). The Lord has provided this shield, but He does not intend for His children to spend their days dodging darts. Great authority has been delivered to all believers, more than enough to take the day, every day, for the Kingdom of God. "And when he had called unto him his twelve disciples, he gave them power against unclean spirits, to cast them out, and to heal all manner of sickness and all manner of disease" (Matthew 10:1; also see Luke 9:1, 10:19)

When Jesus rose into the heavens, He did not leave His followers comfortless, but sent "the promise of my Father" by which all believers are "endued with power from on high" (Luke 24:49; also see Acts 1:8; Luke 4:36; Matthew 28:19).

The power of praise should not be overlooked while taking inventory of the stockpile of spiritual weaponry. By the power of high praise, the righteous executes vengeance upon the heathen and punishments upon the people. They bind wicked kings with chains, and their nobles with fetters of iron. They execute judgments written. (Psalms 149:6-9; also see Judges 5:2; 2

Chronicles 20:22; Psalms 9:1, 22:22, 34:1). In other words, through high praise, believers "accomplish or enact the settled or established will or intent of God."

As spiritual Israel lifts its voice to give Jesus the high praise that is due His Name, deliverance is present, enemies are defeated, food is provided, jails are broken down, fiery furnaces are cooled off, hungry lions won't eat, barren women give birth, life comes back into dead bodies, and the list goes on (see Hebrews 11). With all the powerful weapons of warfare that God has made accessible to the Church, to every believer in every place, why does Satan still fight to control the day? Why does the adversary still try to dominate with his evil presence? If the devil knows how much power every believer has against him, why make the effort?

As has already been stated, it is the devil's nature to establish his will for each day. He was created to rule the day as the "morning star". In most places, his authority as the first light of day goes unchecked and unchallenged because in most places the true authority, which are the believers, are still asleep while the devil is staking his claims. God's people have the ability to win every skirmish on every front, but the battle for the day is so often lost simply by default.

"And having spoiled principalities and powers, he made a shew of them openly,

34

triumphing over them in it." (Colossians 2:15)

"He that committeth sin is of the devil; for the devil sinneth from the beginning. For this purpose the Son of God was manifested, that he might destroy the works of the devil." (I John 3:8)

According to these scriptures, the devil has been triumphed over, his powers have been spoiled, and his works have been destroyed. This was accomplished by the power of the cross. Believers have been given power and authority over an already conquered devil. Jesus' triumph was our triumph. His victory was our victory. Jesus put Satan under your feet. If he is not still there who let him out? (Genesis 3:15, Luke 10:19, Joshua 10:24, Romans 16:20) One of the devil's most effective deceptions against the Church is to lure us into the battle that belongs to God. Our fight is the "good fight of faith", but the devil attempts to engage us in the Lord's battle. (1 Timothy 6:12, 1 Samuel 17:47) If we can be deceived into trying to accomplish by human effort what only God can do, it places us in an awkward position. This position virtually ties the hands of God from being able to work on our behalf, nullifies our faith, turns our labor into vanity and creates an attitude of weariness that will cause us to "faint in our minds." (Hebrews 12:3) This of course, is his only chance for victory in our life. The devil knows that not even the gates of hell can withstand the "prayers of faith," (Matthew16:18)

The devil's only remaining option is to try to wear us down.

> *"And he shall speak great words against the most High, and shall wear out the saints of the most High, and think to change times and laws: and they shall be given into his hand until a time and times and the dividing of time."* (Daniel 7:25)

End of Night

Throughout the scripture, one example after another is given of angelic intervention in the lives of God's chosen ones. Almost without exception, the angelic activities recorded in the Bible were carried out in the morning. Those that were not completed by the time the sun had risen were at least initiated in what was commonly called the "morning watch", or the fourth watch of the night. "Morning", as mentioned 214 times in the Old Testament alone, is given a literal translation of "daybreak" or "could see".

The Hebrew word for morning is, "boger", meaning "morning though not the period of time before noon. Rather it indicates the point of time at which night is changing to day or at the end of night." The Archangel Lucifer was created with the ability to dazzle. Observe Ezekiel's description:

> *"Thou has been in Eden the garden of God; every precious stone was thy covering, the sardius, topaz, and the diamond, the beryl, the onyx, and the jasper, the sapphire, the emerald and the carbuncle, and gold: the workmanship of thy tabrets and of thy pipes*

> *was prepared in thee in the day that thou was created. Thou art the anointed cherub that covereth; and I have set thee so: thou wast upon the holy mountain of God; thou has walked up and down in the midst of the stones of fire.*" (Ezekiel 28:13-14)

Not only was Lucifer created to dazzle, but he was created also as the cherub that covereth, or the angel that ruled. He was created to rule the day. Lucifer's authority was recognized by all angelic beings and by all of God's creation. Because of his place of authority, one-third of the angels rebelled with him against God. Is it any wonder that Satan still tries to assert the authority that he once had, despite the fact that dominion has been taken from Lucifer and given to the saints? He attempts to rule the day, and he is successful if not challenged by the proper authority.

If believers are to rule the day in their cities, they must challenge and defeat Satan at his point of entry. The Church must assume its place each day as the light of the world before the devil can stake his claim to it. The Psalmist's vision and understanding must challenge the efforts of the Church every day: "I will awaken the dawn" (Psalm 57:8 NIV).

Jesus spoke of the condemnation that men feel because they love the darkness rather than the light. Man is often more comfortable in his flesh at night because of the nature of sin that rules his life. When believers come into the truth, their nature changes so as to love the light (see John 3:19-21). Although our nature changes because of God's light, all too often habits do not change as quickly, if at all. It is possible for a believer's spirit to live in the light while the body still lives in the night. Jesus said, "If a man walk in the night he stumbleth" (John 11:10). The word walk signifies "the whole round of the activities of individual life" (Vine's Expository Dictionary). Spiritual and physical activities must be baptized with the very nature of light in order for an individual to "walk in the spirit", not fulfilling the desire of the flesh. The flip side of not living in the spirit is, then, yielding to the desire of the human nature (see John 12:35-36; Romans 8:1-10; Ephesians 5:8; Galatians 5:16).

The Apostle John shares an embarrassing moment for Jesus' closest friends and fellow laborers. "Early in the morning Jesus stood on the shore, but the disciples did not realize that it was Jesus" (John 21:4 NIV). Why did the disciples not recognize the Lord after all the time they had shared, especially given the familiarity of the circumstances? For the same reason that God's people far too often fail to recognize the countenance and voice of the Lord when He has something special prepared for them. It is because the carnal man is still living with the habits of darkness. The Bible does not say why the disciples did not realize that it was Jesus on the shore, but we do know that they had been up all night fishing. While God never condemned fishing, late night activities still keep some from realizing that God is calling His people to a place of prayer in the early hours of each morning.

At a ministerial conference several years ago I bumped into a pastor who had preached at a crusade in Ethiopia that I had attended the year before. He began telling me about a beautiful campus that his fellowship had recently acquired on the East coast of America. As he described the facility, the Lord impressed upon me that I should go to this place and pray over it. When the pastor paused I interrupted and shared with him what the Lord had spoken to my spirit. To say the least, he was overjoyed and expressed it then and there. He then told me the rest of the story. For many years, this facility had been a place of occult activity. Satanic rituals where being preformed there up until the time that his group purchased the property, and they could still feel the demonic oppression that had dominated that entire region for decades. The Lord had impressed upon me that the demonic spirit we were going to come against was the spirit that controlled the entire eastern seaboard of America. When our prayer team arrived on site, the atmosphere was charged with great faith. We went right to the place where most of the demonic rituals had occurred, taking authority in the Name of Jesus and praying in the power of the Spirit. After we had prayed that way for a couple of hours, the demonic forces broke rank and started fleeing. For the next hour or so, a spirit of praise was upon the entire prayer team and we all rejoiced in the Lord.

The Board of Directors was having a business meeting on the campus and asked that we come in and share what the Lord had shown us about the place. As I expressed my feelings about what that place had been, the demonic spirit that had prevailed there and the events of the past few hours, the Chairman of the Board of Directors jumped to his feet. "I can tell you exactly when that spirit broke and ran", he said. "We were sitting here going through our business as usual when the Spirit of the Lord fell upon us. Suddenly, as one man, we came to our feet rejoicing as what seemed like a wind of God came blowing through this room. It felt as though that wind was blowing away all demonic spirits that were on this property." When we compared notes, this "wind of God" came at the same time the prayer team had broken through in victory. Long before sunrise the next morning, the prayer team paired up to go on a prayer-walk through each of the buildings and around the property line. We walked around binding demonic spirits from that place and releasing the peace of God to minister there.

Just before sunrise, we assembled in the courtyard of the dorm area. As the sun was rising, we were rejoicing in the victory, which the Lord had given.

We later discovered that as we were rejoicing, two earthquakes, each measuring over 3.0, hit that exact location. The place where we prayed together was literally, shaken.

Two years later, the Lord sent me to a prayer conference in Indiana. The pastor there told me about a witch who had come to God in his church. She had told him that she was from the East coast area and that most of the witches she knew from home were in the process of moving. She told her pastor that the witches on the East coast had lost their spiritual power about two years before and they had not been able to get it back so they were all relocating.

Life Patterns

The Word of God exposes a great number of "patterns" of lifestyle from which God chose the people He used. All are somewhat different. Some are altogether different. Some lived in a palace while others had no home at all. Some were eloquent speakers and some had speech impediments. While some had great wealth and influence, others lived in abject poverty. Men, who were educated by the highest standards of their day, were used by God as well as those deemed as being ignorant and unlearned. The one common element in the life of every great man or woman of God in the Scripture is early morning prayer. It is a practice, which makes it easy to fulfill the command of Romans 12:1-2.

> *"I beseech you, therefore, brethren, by the mercies of God, that ye present your bodies a living sacrifice, holy, acceptable unto God, which is your reasonable service. And be not conformed to this world: but be ye transformed by the renewing of your mind, that ye may prove what is that good, and acceptable, and perfect will of God."*

We must come to understand that through the act of submission and presentation to God, the door is opened for the will of God to be manifested in our everyday lives. Such submission can only be accomplished through obedience to Christ's words in Matthew 16:24,

> *"If any man will come after me, let him deny himself, and take up his cross, and follow me."*

Denying self is essential to allowing God's will to be established in our lives. Two wills cannot control one life, for no man can serve two masters. Therefore, we must die out to self, and that only happens by following Jesus' example of prayer in the Garden of Gethsemane. Christ's agonizing battle over whose will would dominate ended only after several bouts of intense prayer. This type of blood-sweating prayer must become the daily habit of those who would manifest the will of God in their lives. Jesus Christ, as King of Kings, would also be the "Pattern of Patterns". His life and ministry was built on much prayer. The Gospels make it evident that His example of prayer was as follows: "...rising up a great while before day, he went out and departed into a solitary place, and there prayed." (Mark 1:35).

From cover to cover, the Bible is filled with scores of examples of men and women who were mightily used by God. The Bible also indicates that these spiritual warriors made it a habit of rising up before the break of day to commune with God, bind evil spirits, and get their marching orders for the day. This same pattern of early morning prayer was also found in the lives of early Christian reformers and evangelists who have had a great impact on our modern world.

Abraham, whom the Apostle Paul referred to as "the father of faith", was in the habit of rising before sunrise to build an altar and seek after God. According to Genesis 19:27: "And Abraham gat up early in the morning to the place where he stood before the Lord." This verse not only refers to the time of prayer, but also "the place", underscoring the consistency of Abraham's early morning prayer life. Even on what was probably the worst day of his life, Abraham still met God in the morning hours.

> *"[Abraham] rose up early in the morning saddled his ass, and took two of his young men with him, and Isaac his son, and clave the wood for the burnt offering, and rose up and went unto the place of which God had told him."* (Genesis 22:3)

From the beginning of their relationship, Abraham committed himself to obeying the voice of God no matter what it might cost. The first orders that God gave this seventy-year-old man were to leave the comforts of home and go wander in the hot burning desert. Abraham was accustomed to sacrifice. It was as simple as, "God would speak and Abraham would obey." The "father of faith" was so dedicated to obeying God's instructions that the Lord had to speak to him twice to stop him for sacrificing his own son.

As a type and shadow of things to come, God sent Moses into Pharaoh's presence to demand the release of Israel from bondage. In accordance with so many other spiritual activities recorded in Scripture, Moses was sent to confront the Egyptian king just before sunrise. Had this occurred only once, or if there were no other Biblical references regarding the hand of God at this time of day, then perhaps this would be somewhat insignificant. However, this is not the case. The Bible is very specific concerning the time of day at which God intended for Moses to approach Pharaoh. This happened not once, but throughout the deliverance of God's people (see: Exodus 7:15, 8:20, 9:13). It is also interesting to note that many years before Moses' birth, God dealt with another Pharaoh through Joseph, but still in the early morning hours (Genesis 41:8). Two different Pharaohs, two different generations, two different men of God, but still God chose the same time of day. Could it be that God is showing his people an extremely powerful principle of prayer? If God's people would fashion their prayer lives after this pattern, what results would follow? God wants to show the world another great deliverance, but perhaps He is waiting for someone to get up, get in the devil's face, and command him, "Let my family go!"

There are many "Pharaohs" in the spirit realm that are holding people in bondage. The Word of God still echoes, "Rise up early in the morning and stand before Pharaoh, and say to him, Thus saith the Lord God of the Hebrews, Let my people go" (Exodus 9:13). The description

46

"perfect and upright" was given to only one man in the Bible. Job, referred to by God as "my servant", has the distinct honor of having an entire book of the Bible dedicated to him and bearing his name. There may be several reasons why Job was selected to serve the Lord in the capacity to which he was called. His life certainly seemed to be beyond reproach.

Job chapter one and verse five gives more than a glimpse into the character of Job and the pattern of his life.

"Job...rose up early in the morning and offered burnt offerings. Thus did Job continually."

The fact that Job did this "continually" is most likely why he was titled "perfect and upright". What an awesome pattern for anyone wanting to be used of God!

As the new leader of Israel, Joshua had some mighty big shoes to fill. The only way he could possibly succeed was to follow the example of his predecessor, Moses. The avenue to God's anointing and directions had been lain out before him from the time of Israel's deliverance from bondage. Therefore, as Joshua assumed his responsibilities, he began by rising early, before sunrise, and seeking the face of God (see Joshua 3:1). God honored Joshua's commitment to early morning prayer, and said to him, "This day will I begin to magnify thee in the sight of all Israel, that they may know that, as I was with Moses, so I will be with thee" (Joshua 3:7).

What day was "this day"? It was the day in which Joshua committed to a life of rising early in the morning to seek the face of God. God's Word and His promises are as good today as they were when they were first given. What God promised to do for Joshua, He will certainly do for all others who make and keep the same commitment to early morning prayer. On the day of our commitment to a lifestyle of rising before the sun to seek after the mind of God, He has promised, "This day will I begin to magnify thee...that they may know that...I will be with thee".

Joshua's entire life and ministry was built upon a lifestyle that included rising early to pray for God's direction and deliverance. He carried this foundation of prayer into every battle, every judgment, and every decision of his leadership. This lifestyle of prayer brought him and his people through every battle with little or no casualties. Early morning prayer exposed the sin before every judgment of God, and as a result, no innocent people were destroyed. Early morning prayer gave Joshua clear direction in every command decision for God's people. God's word to Joshua in Joshua 1:8 was, "thou shalt make thy way prosperous, and then thou shalt have good success." By following Moses' pattern of prayer, Joshua made his own way prosperous, and God gave him good success.

The walls of Jericho could not withstand the mighty assault of early morning prayer. Joshua followed the directions from the Lord:

"Joshua rose early in the morning and the priests took up the ark of the Lord. And seven priests bearing seven trumpets of rams' horns before the ark of the Lord went on continually, and blew with the trumpets: and the armed men went before them; but the reward came after the ark of the Lord, the priests going on, and blowing with the trumpets. And the second day, they compassed the city once, and returned into the camp: so they did six days. And it came to pass on the seventh day, that they rose early about the dawning of the day, and compassed the city after the same manner seven times: only on that day they compassed the city seven times." (Joshua 6:12-15)

What was the result of this sacrifice of early morning obedience to the Word of God? The walls came down, and the chosen people of God were victorious. Jacob caught a glimpse of heaven just before sunrise, and the hectic activities that surrounded the Throne of God seem to have scared the wits out of him. He saw angels coming and going from the presence of God into the earth to fulfill their orders for the day. It so deeply affected Jacob that when the sun came up, he built an altar and established that place as a memorial to be revisited (see Genesis 28:11-19). Jacob named this place "Bethel" meaning "the house of God". Many years later, when Jacob was in the greatest distress of his life, he made his way back to Bethel where God touched him and changed not only his name, but his nature as well. Jacob's vision appears to be the same type of activity referenced in the book of Job:

> *"Now there was a day when the sons of God came to present themselves before the Lord, and Satan came also among them"* (Job 1:6).

Throughout the Word of God, the break of day is the predominant time of angelic activity. Another example of this principle is recounted in Genesis when angels rescued Lot from the judgment of God at the break of day. The NIV account reads,

> *"With the coming of dawn, the angels urged Lot"* (Genesis 19:15).

Hannah looked the same as most of the other women who crowded into the temple for sacrifice and prayer. Maybe her prayer was a little longer. Maybe her desire was a bit stronger. Maybe her body language suggested a deeper intensity than most, but it is doubtful that Hannah could have been picked out of a line-up, especially by an old blind priest. But something about Hannah stood out to God. Intense desperation played a major role in God answering Hannah's request for a child. There was another element to Hannah's prayer, however, that may have been of little or no consequence if this characteristic was not mentioned in so many other Biblical passages.

According to additional references, Hannah's prayer took place in the early morning hours. Regardless of how much Hannah's appearance may have favored most other women in the altar that day, the Word says, "God remembered her" (see I Samuel 1:19).

Jesus' promise in Matthew 6:33 reads, "Seek ye first the Kingdom of God, and his righteousness, and all these things shall be added unto you." In order for all of "these things" to be added, there must be an act on the part of the seeker. Primarily, this act is to seek "the Kingdom of God, and his righteousness". The day ought to begin with seeking God so that His promises in this verse can be fulfilled in our lives.

The Psalmist agrees:

"Oh God, thou art my God; early will I seek thee." (Psalm 63:1)

"I rise before Dawn and cry for help; I have put my hope in your word." (Psalm 119:147 NIV)

"But I cry to you for help, O Lord; in the morning my prayer comes before you." (Psalm 88:13 NIV)

"My voice shalt thou hear in the morning O Lord; in the morning will I direct my prayer unto thee, and will look up." (Psalm 5:3)

Isaiah's declaration should inspire anyone to seek the face of God at daybreak. The benefit to those who seek Him early is multifold. Much is promised to those who will commit to continual early morning prayer, including instruction, understanding, the wisdom of God, the right words for the right occasion, and much more (see Isaiah 50:4).

Another great benefit to seeking God at daybreak is found in the book of Ecclesiastes 11:6 and Isaiah 17:11. "In the morning sow thy seed" because "in the morning shalt thou make thy seed flourish." Jesus informed us that "the seed" is the Word of God (Luke 8:11). Therefore, if we sow the Word of Faith in the morning God will cause that Word to flourish. As we pray God's Word and speak out His promises, God will cause that word to have dominion.

> *"So shall my word be that goeth forth out of my mouth: it shall not return unto me void, but it shall accomplish that which I please, and it shall prosper in the thing whereto I sent it."* (Isaiah 55:11)

> *"And very early in the morning the first day of the week, they came unto the sepulcher at the rising of the sun"* (Mark 16:2)

When Mary arrived at the tomb at the rising of the sun, she really got there at the "rising of the Son." This woman with a soiled reputation had an experience with God unparalleled in all of history. Mary caught up with God in His dressing room, after His resurrection but before His translation or transformation. She touched God between dispensations. Mary grabbed hold of God in a time and place in which there was no designated approach to God. Jesus had to actually tell Mary not to touch Him, but it was too late. She had already taken hold of His feet and was not about to let go until she was sent on a mission for the Lord. If we seek God in the early morning hours, we will see Him in a light that no one else can. In fact, "in the morning then ye shall see the glory of the Lord" (Exodus 16:7). How much do we miss simply because we get there too late?

Morning By Morning

The prophet Ezekiel testifies, "in the morning came the word of the Lord unto me" (Ezekiel 12:8). This promise is not just to one Old Testament prophet, but "every morning doth he bring his judgment to light" (Zephaniah 3:5). The "judgment" referred to by Zephaniah is not the fire and brimstone judgment that may rush to mind. Rather, God is speaking of His testament or will. As we give ourselves to consistent daybreak prayer, light is shed upon the will of God for our lives. God does not delight in concealing His plan for our lives. He does not play hide-and-seek with His people, hiding His will expecting us to find it on our own. Many confess to agonizing in prayer, seeking the will of God, only to come away feeling as if the heavens were shut and that God was nowhere to be found. God desires us to know His will, and has given us directions to find Him: "I love them that love me; and those that seek me early shall find me" (Proverbs 8:17). God is easily discovered by those willing to seek Him at the right time.

One morning the Lord spoke to me and said, "I want you to go find Bill." Bill was a young man that God had brought into our lives several years before. The Lord had allowed me to influence him, and he was becoming not only a fine Christian but a great soul-winner and preacher. Bill had been like a son to Karen and me. In fact, I do not believe that we could have loved him any more if he had been our birth-child. But, Bill was gone. This young man had been overtaken by sin and fell prey to Satan's devices. For over two years we had not heard a word from Bill and the last we knew of him, he had moved into a major metropolitan area of over four million people. We had spent many hours praying for and weeping over the loss of this soul. So, when the Lord impressed upon me to find Bill, I was both excited by the prospect of being reunited with him and perplexed as to how I could accomplish this task.

It was early afternoon when the voice of the Lord came to me again concerning Bill. I must go now. I drove to the end of our street and stopped. I prayed to God to direct me on this mission and waited until I felt the prompting of the Holy Spirit to turn right (a direction that I would not have chosen). At every crossroad and intersection, I waited for God to give me a nudge in the right direction. After a few miles, I was turning on roads that I had never been on or knew existed. I was traveling further from town down a lonely country road when the Lord instructed me to turn left at the next driveway. I passed the driveway before I saw it. It hardly qualified as a driveway as it was more of an overgrown dirt trail leading into a field with no house in sight. After staring down the dirt trail for a few minutes, trying to figure out if I had heard from God or not about all of this, I went on. I could not see a dwelling of any kind until I topped the huge hill I saw from the road. There to my surprise was a nice home with several cars parked in the yard. When I stepped onto the front porch a lady came to the door and I began. "You don't know me", I explained, "but I'm looking for Bill." "He's not here right now," she answered. "He works with my husband. That's his car over there, but they won't be home until dark." "Thank you, thank you, thank you", I shouted. To say the least, I was elated. I placed a note on Bill's car asking him to call me, then left, planning to come back before dark. It took a few minutes to get back to the main highway, and when I stopped at the intersection, I felt that familiar nudge from God. "Don't go home yet, you're not finished," the Spirit whispered. "But, God," I complained, "it will be almost five hours before Bill gets home from work. What do you want me to do?" "Turn left" was His only instruction. A couple of miles or so down the road was a small convenience store. I felt the leading of the Spirit to pull in, but nothing more. I was sitting in my car in the middle of the parking lot, feeling more than a little conspicuous, and wondered what I should do next.

Several years before, I had concluded that it is always the will of God to get a diet coke so I decided to get some fuel and a soft drink. A few minutes later, standing at the counter, looking through the plate-glass window, I saw it. That old car I had left a note on just fifteen or twenty minutes earlier was sitting at the same gas pump as my car. And there was Bill standing by his car putting gas in the tank. I quickly paid and walked out the door. I had taken only a few steps toward Bill when he looked up and saw me. His eyes filled with tears as he ran to me, wrapping his arms around me he began to sob and repent to God. Within a few minutes, my prodigal son had prayed through to a renewed relationship with Jesus.

The woman I had spoken with at the house did not know that her husband and Bill were going to be getting off work early that day, but Jesus did. In fact, Jesus ignited the fuse early that morning that set in order the sequence of events that would bring Bill and me together that afternoon. If I had not been at the throne of God early that morning I would not have been at that store to meet Bill and bring him home to the Father.

It must be stated that there is nothing wrong with praying at night. In fact, prayer at anytime is good. Yet, there is quite a difference between what and how we pray at night compared to what and how we pray in the morning (unless our night prayer is a follow-up built on a life of consistent early morning prayer). Night prayers are normally filled with repentance, "I'm sorry", missed opportunities and regrets unless they are built on the foundation of morning prayer. Morning prayers are full of worship, praise, direction, guidance, and forgiving others. Therefore, there is greater power and, as we have seen, there are proven results as a derivative of praying early in the morning. Is it any wonder the Psalmist proclaimed: "Weeping may endure for a night, but joy cometh in the morning"? (Psalm 30:5)

Like all decisions of great significance, application of early morning prayer must be consistent. The manna must be gathered morning by morning before the sun comes up to melt it away. Moses' commandment concerning the manna was that none should be left on the ground. They quickly discovered that manna left on the ground until after sunrise would melt. And if they tried to gather enough to last for more than one day it would be filled with worms and stink (see Exodus 16:19-21). In terms of prayer, we must gather the manna morning by morning before the sun comes up and the richness of God's provision is lost to the day. In addition, it is important to recognize the futility of expecting what we may gather from Church on Sunday to last us through the week. As the physical manna had to be gathered "morning by morning", the spiritual manna must be gathered every morning before the day begins.

This is consistent with God's way, for from the beginning, God established His time of fellowship with man in the cool of the day. Is it not amazing that the coolest part of the day is just before the rising of the sun? The prophet Amos commanded God's people to bring their sacrifices every morning (Amos 4:4). Moses instructed the Israelites to build the church by a life of continued offerings "morning by morning"

(Exodus 36:3 NIV). "It is of the Lord's mercies that we are not consumed, because his compassions fail not. They are new every morning: great is thy faithfulness". (Lamentations 3:22-23)

Benefits of Early Morning Prayer

Consistent participation in the act and spirit of Early Morning Prayer will eradicate from your life the things that create the majority of all spiritual inconsistencies. Almost all of the works of the flesh that continually disrupt the flow of God can be eliminated totally by a commitment to diligently seeking God at the break of each new day. When every day is begun with a fresh pursuit of the presence of God, none of the inconsistencies of human endeavor will be able to dominate.

Prayerlessness

It is absolutely mind boggling to discover how many Christians live under a heavy weight of condemnation simply because they do not engage themselves in daily prayer. A startling percentage of Christian laity attempt to live in spiritual victory without it. Even more disturbing is the fact that a very high percentage of Christian ministers and Church leadership live almost everyday with the accusing voice of prayerlessness.

"Ye lust, and have not: ye kill, and desire to have, and cannot obtain: ye fight and war, yet ye have not, because ye ask not." (James 4:2)

Consistent participation with God in the act of early morning prayer will totally destroy the condemnation of prayerlessness. Beginning each day with prayer certainly fulfills the "seek ye first" admonition of Jesus. (Matthew 6:33)

When developing an early morning prayer-life definite phases of prayer become obvious. These phases of prayer are easy to work through by understanding that these phases exist. The four phases of prayer seem to coincide with the amount of time given to the deeper "Dimensions of Prayer".

Phases of Prayer:

1. **Faith** - enthusiasm & excitement because of the newness

2. **Commitment** – duty praying – the right thing to do

3. **Believe** – result-oriented praying– prayers are being answered

4. **Relationship** - fellowship with God

Experience indicates that the more time and depth given to the fourth dimension of prayer, the quicker "Relationship Praying" develops.

Pride/Selfishness

"If my people, which are called by my name, shall humble themselves, and pray, and seek my face, and turn from their wicked ways; then will I hear from heaven, and will forgive their sin, and will heal their land." (2 Chronicles 7:14)

The "Harvest of Lost Souls" is the final outcome of this promise. But there is a definite process of succession, which must be diligently followed in order to obtain this promise. Before an atmosphere of "harvest" can be developed, the Church must be "revived." Since the "Church" is made up of individual members, each individual in the body must have a personal "revival." "Revival" is a result of "turning from wicked ways" or repentance.

"...all should come to repentance." (II Peter 3:9)

"the goodness of God leadeth thee to repentance?" (Romans 2:4)

"For godly sorrow worketh repentance to salvation..." (II Corinthians 7:10)

"if God peradventure will give them repentance" (II Timothy 2:25)

True repentance is change. "Turning from wicked ways" is the result of spiritual hunger (seeking His glory or seeking His face). Seeking is the result of "consistency in prayer." Consistent prayer is built upon the foundation of "humility." Prayerlessness, sweet and simple, is a result of pride. Every day that is started without prayer is equivalent to saying to God, "I don't need you today." Humility is developed through understanding that we belong to God.

"What? know ye not that your body is the temple of the Holy Ghost which is in you, which ye have of God, and ye are not your own? For ye are bought with a price: therefore glorify God in your body, and in your spirit, which are God' s." (I Corinthians 6:19-20)

"Know ye that the LORD he is God: it is he that hath made us, and not we ourselves; we are his people, and the sheep of his pasture." (Psalm 100:3)

Inconsistency (Unfaithfulness)

The lives of so many Christians are littered with inconsistencies. Being faithful to obligations and commitments has for some reason become passé. It appears that too many believers take a nonchalant attitude toward their commitments. Dedication to early morning prayer will show up in every other area of life.

Abraham, the Father of (the) Faith(ful), provides plenty of evidence that commitment to seeking God early each morning will develop an attitude of faithfulness in every area of life.

"And Abraham gat up early in the morning to the place where he stood before the LORD:" (Genesis 19:27)

"that he (Abraham) might be the father of all them that believe" (Romans 4:11)

"Who then is a faithful and wise servant, whom his lord hath made ruler over his household, to give them meat in due season?" (Matthew 24:45)

"His lord said unto him, Well done, thou good and faithful servant: thou hast been faithful over a few things, I will make thee ruler over many things: enter thou into the joy of thy lord." (Matthew 25:21)

"Moreover it is required in stewards, that a man be found faithful." (I Corinthians 4:2)

Slothfulness

Spiritual indifference has definitely reached epidemic proportion in post-modern Christianity. Hot pursuit of God has been replaced by an attitude of self-indulgence. However, a consistent commitment to a lifestyle of rising early each morning to commune with God restores spiritual hunger. This type of commitment also restores submission to God and therefore, obedience to the voice of the Spirit. A slothful attitude will completely erode by actively seeking God each morning.

> *"Then, knowing what lies ahead for you, you won' t becane bored with being a Christian nor become spiritually dull and indifferent, but you will be anxious to follow the example of those who receive all that God has promised them because of their strong faith and patience."* (Hebrews 6:12 TLB)

Lack of Commitment

Prayerlessness will always produce a lack of follow-through in the life of any believer. The act of early morning praying will develop a resolve to see the "Word of Faith" flourish.

> *"He also that received seed among the thorns is he that heareth the word; and the care of this world, and the deceitfulness of riches, choke the word, and he becometh unfruitful."* (Matthew 13:22)

> *"And the cares of this world, and the deceitfulness of riches, and the lusts of other things entering in, choke the word, and it becometh unfruitful."* (Mark 4:19)

These two separate but related Scripture references concerning "the seed", "the sower" and "the ground" bring to light two different yet similar schools of thought. Matthew's record of this parable by using the word "he" indicates that the ground becomes incapable of producing fruit. This particular Scriptural text is an indictment against Christians who, through prayerlessness, have become too dull and insensitive to allow any "Word of Faith" to be productive in their life.

Mark, on the other hand, informs his readers that, "it" (the seed or the Word) becomes unfruitful. By using the word "becometh" both writers are expressing the idea of a process. While Matthew seems to be concerned with the person ("he") becoming unable to reap any benefit from the Word, Mark describes a situation where it becomes increasingly probable for "good ground" or "faithful Christians" to lose their ability to receive certain seed with operative faith.

Discord

One of the devil's most effective weapons against the child of God is in trying to make them feel unattached to and/or out-of-step with their spiritual authority (which is usually a pastor) or with the rest of the body. When feelings of separation are routinely accepted as normal, it is impossible to live in the "unity of the faith." Jesus admonished His followers to agree together in prayer, promising that anything they asked in the spirit of unity would come to pass. (Matthew 18:19)

Discord is dispelled by exercising the "spirit of unity." A true "spirit of unity" can only be sustained through consistently abiding with Christ. When any number of people is yielded to God every morning in prayer, absolutely no discord can exist between them because *"he that is joined unto the Lord is one spirit."* (1 Corinthians 6:17)

Unbelief

Early morning praying in the power of the Holy Spirit on a consistent basis will overcome doubt by strengthening the believer's faith.

> *"...building up yourselves on your most holy faith, praying in the Holy Ghost..."* (Jude 1:20)

The berating voice of condemnation is probably the most powerful ingredient of unbelief. It takes more energy to un-believe than it does to believe because *"God hath dealt to every man the measure of faith."* (Romans 12:3) But personal condemnation empowers the "accuser of the brethren" in his efforts to destroy the believer's confidence in God.

> *"For if our heart condemn us, God is greater than our heart, and knoweth all things. 21 Beloved, if our heart condemn us not, then have we confidence toward God."* (I John 3:20-21)

By beginning every new day seeking the Kingdom of heaven and His righteousness, the voice of condemnation is greatly disarmed. By a continual application of early morning prayer, faith is built up, condemnation is cast out, confidence is restored and unbelief is cast down. The process of building faith is executed through a commitment of starting each day with Christ and abiding in Him throughout the day.

Metamorphosis of Faith

1. Believing that God Can!!!
2. Believing that God Will!!!

(As condemnation gives way to confidence.)

3. God can through me!!!!
4. God will through me!!!!

"There is therefore now no condemnation to them which are in Christ Jesus, who walk not after the flesh, but after the Spirit." (Romans 8:1)

Blessings from Early Morning Prayer

The lone, simple act of obedience to the Word of God will, without fail, produce powerful results. Samuel's understanding of obedience allowed God to do for him what God desires to do for all who are faithful to His Word. The Bible explains why Samuel was feared as one of the greatest Prophets who ever lived:

> *"And Samuel grew, and the LORD was with him, and did let none of his words fall to the ground."* (1 Samuel 3:19)

Whatever Samuel spoke, God would make sure that it came to pass. It was the prophet's grasp on the principle of submission and obedience that enabled him to walk in a place of great spiritual authority. Samuel tried to teach King Saul this principle but to no avail. Hear his words:

> *"...Hath the LORD as great delight in burnt offerings and sacrifices, as in obeying the voice of the LORD? Behold, to obey is better*

than sacrifice, and to hearken than the fat of rams." (I Samuel 15:22)

Obedience is the life-giving force that resurrects dead faith. The act of obeying adds works to faith thus bringing it to life, and living faith pleases God. (See James 2:20, Hebrews 11:6) The Apostle James basically teaches the essentiality of taking action on the Word of God in order to produce positive spiritual results in life. By taking action and being a doer of the Word, the promises of God become a reality of life.

Simple obedience to God's Word by consistently praying early each morning will give life to many promises and blessings. These promises and blessings of God will begin to be manifested in the lives of those who practice submission and obedience.

"And it shall come to pass, if thou shalt hearken diligently unto the voice of the LORD thy God, to observe and to do all his commandments which I command thee this day, that the LORD thy God will set thee on high above all nations of the earth: 2 And all these blessings shall come on thee, and overtake thee, if thou shalt hearken unto the voice of the LORD thy God." (Deuteronomy 28:1-2)

Promised Blessings from Early Morning Prayer

Direction for Life

One of the greatest blessings that can be derived from faithful obedience to early morning prayer is finding God's direction for life. Since the steps of the righteous are ordered of the Lord, knowing what those steps are and where those steps will lead is paramount. This type of knowledge is granted to those who seek Him early.

Because of traditional mindsets, it is easy to restrict the ways in which God can speak. God may use any number of methods to give specific direction to those who obey His Word by praying in the early morning hours. Regardless of how the information comes, scriptural evidence is clear on this one point: it will come.

> *"God, who at sundry times and in divers manners spake in time past unto the fathers by the prophets, 2 Hath in these last days spoken unto us by his Son, whom he hath appointed heir of all things, by whom also he made the worlds..."* (Hebrews 1:1-2)

> *"My sheep hear my voice..."* (John 10:27)

> *"He that hath an ear, let him hear what the Spirit saith unto the churches..."* (Revelation 2:7)

From time to time, God speaks to His people by varying means. The Word of God is clear on these three points:

1. God has spoken and continues to speak to His people.
2. His people recognize His voice regardless of how He speaks.
3. It takes a spiritually sensitive ear to know when God is speaking.

God may speak through a *still small voice* but then again, He may speak through the *whirlwind*. God may speak through a simple impression that comes into your human spirit. God speaks to His people through His Word, both written and spoken. God can speak through His ministers and His saints. God still chooses the medium of preaching to save those who believe. Several spiritual gifts enumerated by the Apostle Paul were spoken. God still gives direction through many various methods. The greatest need of the hour is not for God to speak but for His people to develop an ear that is spiritually sensitive to His voice.

Direction came to King David when he was praying early in the morning through the Man of God.

> *"For when David was up in the morning, the word of the LORD came unto the prophet Gad, David's seer, saying..."* (II Samuel 24:11)

Although it is not clear if God spoke to Ezekiel with a loud audible voice, a still small voice or an impression in his spirit, God ultimately spoke.

"And in the morning came the word of the LORD unto me." (Ezekiel 12.8)

Every morning God teaches a Bible class. The most effective Bible College that anyone could ever attend would be to sit in the presence of the "Author and Finisher of our faith." (Hebrews 12:2)

"The just LORD is in the midst thereof; ..every morning doth he bring his judgment to light..." (Zephaniah 3:5)

"The Lord GOD hath given me the tongue of the learned, that I should know how to speak a word in season to him that is weary: he wakeneth morning by morning, *he wakeneth mine ear to hear as the learned."* (Isaiah 50:4)

Being Used of God

Jesus explained to His disciples a powerful principle about being used in His kingdom. It seems that God does not choose His instruments based on the same merits that men do. God's choice is not based as much on what talent or ability someone may have to offer as it does on someone simply being available.

"For the kingdom of heaven is like unto a man that is an householder, which went out early in the morning to hire labourers into his vineyard." (Matthew 20:1)

God goes out early in the morning to find the workers that He will use in His service. If you want to be used of God you must be at the labor-pool early in the morning when God is looking for those He will use for the day.

"At dawn he appeared again in the temple courts, where all the people gathered around him, and he sat down to teach them." (John 8:2)

Even a casual reading of the Bible provides enough evidence to discover that those who were mightily used of God sought Him early.

Following the example of his predecessor, Joshua rose up early in the morning to follow the Lord's instructions;

"And the LORD said unto Joshua, This day will I begin to magnify thee in the sight of all Israel, that they may know that, as I was with Moses, so I will be with thee." (Joshua 3:7)

"And Joshua rose early in the morning, and the priests took up the ark of the LORD." (Joshua 6:12)

"And Joshua rose up early in the morning, and numbered the people, and went up, he and the elders of Israel, before the people to Ai." (Joshua 8:10)

David, a man set apart by several distinctions, including slaying the giant and being called "a man after God's own heart", sought the Lord early.

"...I myself will awake early."
"...I will awaken the dawn." (NIV)
(Psalm 57:8)

"O God, thou art my God; early will I seek thee:" (Psalm 63:1)

Why should "I rise before dawn and cry for help"? Because, "I have put my hope in your word." (Psalm 119:147 NIV)

One of God's most educated and eloquent prophets realized that he could not rely upon natural abilities to do the work of God. Isaiah understood that there was a time and place to present himself before the Lord for optimum benefit.

"With my soul have I desired thee in the night; yea, with my spirit within me will I seek thee early:

WHY????

"for when thy judgments are in the earth, the inhabitants of the world will learn righteousness." (Isaiah 26:9)

When the devil accused God of having a hedge built around Job and all that belonged to him, God could not deny it. In fact, God's response and the ensuing discussion concerning Job and his family indicate that Satan's perspective seemed to be extremely accurate. The only question about the devil's concept would be "what actually built the hedge?" According to the Angel that was sent to Cornelius, it is the act of prayer coupled with sacrifice that performs the construction work. (Acts 10:3-4) And the life of Job was a life of early morning prayer and sacrifice.

"And it was so, ...that Job ...rose up early in the morning, and offered burnt offerings ...Thus did Job continually." (Job 1:5)

Early Morning Prayer is the "Key"

The chambers and treasuries of the Lord's house are accessible to those who have the key and use it. The charge of the key was given to those who made the house of God the center of their life and would come into it early every morning.

"They would spend the night stationed around the house of God, because they had

*to guard it; and they had charge of the key
for opening it each morning."* (1 Chronicles
9:26 NIV)

Building a Relationship with God

Adam, where are you???

Adam's heart must have run the gauntlet of
emotional extremes when he heard the voice of
the Lord calling his name. Trying his best to hide
from his Creator, Adam apparently never
suspected that God would come searching for
him. It seems that Adam did not realize just how
important their relationship had become to God.
This event exemplifies the extent to which God
will go in order to salvage a relationship that has
been forged through intimate early morning
fellowship.

The message comes through loud and clear:
once a relationship with God has been developed,
if something should happen that would cause you
to stumble, God will come looking for you. God
will not leave you in your dilemma wondering if
He still loves you. Rather, He will come to rescue
you and do everything within His power to
restore the relationship that has been
established.

*"And they heard the voice of the LORD God
walking in the garden in the cool of the day:
and Adam and his wife hid themselves from
the presence of the LORD God amongst the
trees of the garden. 9 And the LORD God*

called unto Adam, and said unto him, Where art thou?" (Genesis 3:8-9)

Abraham, Friend of God

In the process of obtaining the position of the "Father of Faith", Abraham became a "Friend of God." The position became Abraham's when he initially obeyed the voice of God and left Ur. The relationship developed Abraham's consistency in the act of early morning prayer.

"And Abraham gat up early in the morning to the place where he stood before the LORD:" (Genesis 19:27)

Moses Built an Altar Early in the Morning

Deep, lasting relationships are developed through mutual trust. Developing trust involves a process of openness over a period of time. The more transparent you are the less time it takes to build trust thereby building a relationship faster. Moses had just such a relationship with God. It is obvious that from their first encounter at the burning bush until the deliverance of Israel, Moses had developed a deep moral trust in God. It is also obvious that God had concluded that He could put His trust in Moses.

"And be ready in the morning, and come up in the morning unto mount Sinai, and present thyself there to me in the top of the mount. 4 ...and Moses rose up early in the

morning, and went up unto mount Sinai, as the LORD had commanded him,..." (Exodus 34:2 & 4)

Mary Saw Him First

The dispensation of Law ended with the death of the "Lamb of God". Jesus told the High Priest that there would never be a need for another lamb to be slain because the lamb that was being offered would cover the sins of all men, forever. The dispensation of grace had not yet begun. It would be introduced with the outpouring of the Holy Ghost on the Day of Pentecost. There was no designated approach to God, but Mary desired Him. She longed to be with Jesus, and her craving for His presence brought her to the place where His body lay in the grave.

Even with no open avenue of approach to the presence of God, Mary found a way in. While Jesus was telling Mary not to touch Him, she was holding on to His feet. How could this be? Simply because Mary was there at the right time. The right time was then and is now at the rising of the sun. It is possible to find a way into the presence of God by just showing up at daybreak. Mary established a special relationship with God by seeking Him out before the day began.

"And very early in the morning the first day of the week, they came unto the sepulchre at the rising of the sun." (Mark 16:2)

Ananias

The most remarkable biblical illustration of mutual trust between God and man is found in the ninth chapter of the book of Acts. Found hidden among the miraculous conversion of Saul of Tarsus is the story of a man in which God has extreme confidence. God apparently knows Ananias well enough to speak for him. Because of the deep relationship established through consistent prayer, God was able to commit Ananias to a potentially dangerous situation, totally confident that Ananias would follow through.

> *"And there was a certain disciple at Damascus, named Ananias; and to him said the Lord in a vision, Ananias. And he said, Behold, I am here, Lord. 11 And the Lord said unto him, Arise, and go into the street which is called Straight, and inquire in the house of Judas for one called Saul, of Tarsus: for, behold, he prayeth, 12 And hath seen in a vision a man named Ananias coming in, and putting his hand on him, that he might receive his sight."* (Acts 9:10-12)

These several blessings that have been mentioned are not an exhaustive list of what can be obtained through the act of early morning, prayer. These things have been listed simply to whet the appetite for greater spiritual life. The blessings that God will bring into a life that is committed to rising early to seek Him first can never be exhausted.

Staying the Course

Ships have rudders! And there is a very good reason why ships have rudders attached because, as with life, any number of things can happen to knock a sea-faring vessel of course.

When a ship embarks from port, the navigator and/or captain have a definite and predetermined destination in mind. The vessel is set upon a heading that will ultimately bring it safely to harbor in the desired seaport, but from port to port, corrections will be made in the heading so the ship can stay the course. Corrections are not made because of some miscalculation, but rather because winds, tides, currents or some obstacle has forced the ship off course.

Staying the course does not mean that a vessel never gets off course, but when it does veer, corrections are implemented to bring the ship back to proper bearings. Apparently the Apostle Paul understood this principle and realized how it applies to spiritual life. Paul's own testimony states, *"I have fought a good fight, I have finished my course, I have kept the faith."* (2 Timothy 4:7)

The Apostle did not claim to have kept the course, but he was very adamant in his acknowledgment that the course had indeed been finished. This text seems to imply that certain things may happen which cause a life to get off course, but the course can still be finished. The wise man noted in Proverbs 24:16, *"a just man falleth seven times, and riseth up again"*. Paul's assertion that he did *"keep the faith"* evidently supplied the enabling ability for him to *rise up again* so that he could *"finish the course."*

Winds

When winds of adversity blow a ship off its desired heading, only the determined faith and vision of the Captain will continue to bring it back on course. Winds do blow, and that is one of the reasons why ships are built with rudders attached.

> *"But the ship was now in the midst of the sea, tossed with waves: for the wind was contrary."* (Matthew 14:24)

Like the wind described by Matthew, it seems as if most of the winds in life are "contrary". A contrary wind is not necessarily a wind from hell. Any wind that is trying to push the ship in a direction other than the desired port is a contrary wind.

Winds usually come in the form of influence. People, circumstances, temptations, old habits or any other areas of life that serve as a center of influence, can become a contrary wind.

Winds of adversity and resistance must be met with an intentional resolve to persevere. If allowed, contrary winds will cause even a large vessel to stray. Contrary winds are faced almost every day. Resistance is a fact of life for any spiritual pursuit, and it seems especially so in the area of prayer. Diligence is the catchword for spiritual accomplishment. God does reward those who seek Him faithfully.

> *"But without faith it is impossible to please him: for he that cometh to God must believe that he is, and that he is a rewarder of them that diligently seek him."* (Hebrews 11:6)

Tides

> *"...and the care of this world, and the deceitfulness of riches, choke the word, and he becometh unfruitful." (Matthew 13:22)*

The "care of this world" would be an all inclusive description of the tides of life. Daily life abounds with concerns that ebb and flow. If not met with determined strategy, the cares of day-to-day life, though varying, will cause us to become unproductive in spiritual pursuits.

Changing tides are an accepted part of the routine in sea travel. Varying tide patterns from one port to another, although sometimes a bother, are considered to be part of the process of ocean voyage.

Tides are an expected, even a predicted occurrence of life. Although expected, tide patterns must still be calculated into the scheme of navigation. If tide variations are not properly evaluated, they will have devastating effects on the final destination of any sea-faring vessel.

Tides represent the normal routines of life. Although not sinful in and of themselves, the routines that many people follow in daily life are very capable of creating environments that are not conducive to spiritual growth. Something as simple as working overtime, having to work on a rotating shift, or even summer break from school, if not properly considered and planned for can bring a prayer-life to a grinding halt.

Currents

Popular fads, world events, tragedies of life, and other such unexpected but temporary happenings that incite emotional reactions fulfill the definition of currents. It is so easy to be swept into the fray of a strong current, being pulled completely off the desired heading. Often, because of the strength of the current, it is a struggle to get free of its affect. It is possible to be totally aware of the current and how it is changing the direction of spiritual growth and yet feel helpless to be freed of it on our own.

Currents of life usually create a situation where a "life-guard" is needed. "Life-guards" are those people that God places in our life to assist us in overcoming currents and who help supply spiritual direction and insight. God never intended for His children to be self-sufficient. Prayer partners should be sought for and established so that in times of crisis a lifeline can be attached to provide greater security during the voyage. Prayer partners become sounding boards, confidants, and enablers that help us in the recovery process, which also includes the re-establishing of a proper spiritual heading.

Obstacles

Natural elements of normal life produce the greatest amount of spiritual resistance. But natural elements are not the only source of spiritual resistance. Circumstances, other people, or demonic spirits often create obstacles in our path, which can cause us to veer off course. At times, certain obstacles produce situations that necessitate a brief, but intentional, departure from the established route for safety's sake

Shallow water, one of the more obvious concerns of sailing, is most often a concern only when leaving or entering a harbor. As a ship nears a new port-of-call, the captain naturally pays special attention in guiding the vessel, keeping it in the deepest channels possible. But, every good sailor understands that shallow water can also be of grave concern on the open sea. "Shallow water on the open sea?" some may question. The seasoned seafarer responds with a resounding "yes", knowing that every underwater mountain range can present eminent danger. Careful observation exposes a sobering revelation: "Many great lives and ministries have been side-tracked (some permanently) and even destroyed during or near mountain-top experiences." Victories so often produce an intoxicating affect, which has proven to efficiently debilitate righteous judgment.

God is inviting His elect now as He invited the Prophet of old to come into the waters where it is deep enough to swim. (Ezekiel 47:5) Shallow water is a far too perilous place for a child of God to weigh anchor. The Psalmist understood the desire of God to bring His people into the depths of the Spirit realm;

> *"Deep calleth unto deep at the noise of thy waterspouts: all thy waves and thy billows are gone over me." (Psalm 42:7)*

The ocean floor is thoroughly littered with sunken vessels that must be avoided at all cost. A simple glimpse of ships that have failed in their attempt to complete the voyage is one of the most discouraging sights any seafarer could ever see. Every sunken vessel, regardless of the cause, looms as a dreary reminder of what any ship's fate might be.

A great hindrance to the spiritually cautious, who dare to seek the deeper things of God, is the memory of others who tried, failed and were ultimately lost to the sea. The knowledge of fallen comrades should never deter the venture from taking place, but ought to serve as buoys, marking the dangers along the journey.

Certain trade routes are at times strewn with debris and hazards such as icebergs. Most of the devastation that occurs from these perils is a result of what cannot be seen rather than what appears to be the obvious danger. Comprehending the immense jeopardy of the unseen will assist in navigating safely around and through the perils of life.

One of the more discouraging aspects of ocean voyage is the day to day monotony between ports-of-call. Leaving home port is exciting; a new adventure is underway and many positive changes rapidly take place. It is easy on the outset of the trip to see the benefits of the voyage. However, it is difficult, if not impossible, to fully appreciate the progress being made when physical landmarks can no longer be seen.

Embarking upon a daily commitment of early morning prayer is a life-changing decision. In the beginning of any new spiritual endeavor, many changes quickly occur which enhance the resolve to continue. But after the initial experiences of change, staying in the process becomes somewhat tedious when the changes seem to slow down or stop altogether.

It is extremely important to remember that a prayer-life is not an event but rather a continuous journey. A Prayer Voyage will bring us into numerous harbors where great spiritual treasures are introduced into our lives. While in port, being laden with spiritual gifts and cargo, it is easy to stay encouraged about the benefits of living a sacrificial life of early morning prayer. However, those trips between ports, which appear to be uneventful and unfruitful, are the times we must be careful to "keep the faith."

Winds, tides, currents and obstacles seemed to have all come to visit at one time. My life had been bounced from one wave to another for weeks on end. Every schedule had suffered, and my prayer time was so battered that I felt totally ashamed to even approach God. After all, those who knew me well considered me as some sort of an authority on the subject and practice of prayer. "Mr. Prayer", as I had been dubbed by more than a few, had been virtually prayerless for days on end.

I am still not sure whether guilt or desperation convinced me to press on in prayer that morning, but whatever it was, I am eternally grateful that I did. I was busy explaining to God all of the things that had hindered my early morning prayer time and begging forgiveness when God arrested my attention. I saw a vision before me of a graph. On the graph about halfway down on the extreme left side (which was labeled west) appeared a line. The line came from the west and continued approximately a quarter of the way across the graph. As I beheld this sight the voice of the Lord spoke to me and asked, "Which way is the line going?"

After careful examination of the graph I answered, "From west to east." "Does it always go from west to east?" the Lord inquired. "No" I said, "sometimes it drops toward the south and at other times it peaks toward the north, but over all it goes from west to east." "Exactly" replied God, "This is a graph of your prayer-life. At times, your prayer drops off a bit. Still, at other times your prayer-life excels, but overall you are heading in the direction that I have called you to go. When you fall you keep getting back up and that's all I require from you." God continued, "You have been whining about missing a day. I am from everlasting to everlasting, what is twenty-four hours to me? I created the day for you, so quit whining, get over it and get busy praying!"

I now have a better understanding of Paul's statement. I may not always keep the course, but as long as I can keep the faith, I will finish the course. Should I veer off the proper heading and for whatever reason neglect my time of prayer, a new day dawns. And with each new day comes a new Nautical Hour, where I can discover how far I have drifted off course and what corrections I need to make to get back on course, because, I intend to "finish my course".

Scripture References to
Early Morning Prayer

Genesis 19:15
Genesis 19:27-28
Genesis 22:3
Genesis 28:11-13
Genesis 40:6
Genesis 41:8
Exodus 7:15
Exodus 8:20
Exodus 9:13
Exodus 14:24-27
Exodus 16:7
Exodus 16:19-21
Exodus 19:16
Exodus 24:4
Exodus 34:2-4
Joshua 3:1
Joshua 6:12
Joshua 7:14
Joshua 8:10
I Samuel 1:19
II Samuel 24:11
II Kings 19:35
I Chronicles 9:26-27
I Chronicles 23:27-30
Job 1:5-6
Psalm 5:3

Psalm 49:1-14
Psalm 57:8
Psalm 59:16
Psalm 63:1
Psalm 88:13
Psalm 90:14
Psalm 92:1-2
Psalm 119:147
Psalm 143:8
Proverbs 8:17
Ecclesiastes 11:6
Isaiah 17:11
Isaiah 26:9
Isaiah 33:2
Isaiah 50:4
Lamentation 3:22-23
Ezekiel 12:8
Zephaniah 3:5
Matthew 20:1
Mark 1:35
Mark 16:2
Luke 21:38
John 8:2
John 21:4
Acts 5:21

THE END

Ministry Resources

Prayer Conference Schedule
http://www.worldharvestministries.net

Other great books on the subject of "Prayer"

Four Dimensions of Prayer – by Tony Bailey
When Men Pray – by Larry Schoonover

Purchase these and other fine books at:
www.worldharvestministries.net